A CENTURY *of* NEWCASTLE

The old YMCA building (now demolished, later to become Eldon Square shopping complex) close to Grey's Monument, 1972.

A CENTURY *of* NEWCASTLE

JOHN ALEXANDER

SUTTON PUBLISHING

First published in the United Kingdom, in 2000 by
Sutton Publishing Limited · Phoenix Mill
Thrupp · Stroud · Gloucestershire · GL5 2BU

British Library Cataloguing in Publication Data
A catalogue record for this book is available from the British Library.

ISBN 0-7509-2657-0

Front endpaper: Gosforth Park Races, 1948.
Back endpaper: Newcastle Quayside, 1970.
Half title page: A view of Westgate Road, looking up the alleyway of Pink Lane, in 1972. In view is the Visionhire television shop.
Title page: Sidgate Street in the 1960s, alas now demolished.

Published in association with WHSmith

Newcastle children find amusement in the company of a pantomime dame, who is reading from a book of fables, late 1930s.

Typeset in 11/14pt Photina.
Typesetting and origination by
Sutton Publishing Limited.
Printed in Great Britain by
The Bath Press, Bath

Contents

Neville Street, 1970. The popular Douglas Hotel was later demolished to make way for modern buildings.

Britain: A Century of Change

Two women encumbered with gas masks go about their daily tasks during the early days of the war. (*Hulton Getty Picture Collection*)

The sixty years ending in 1900 were a period of huge transformation for Britain. Railway stations, post-and-telegraph offices, police and fire stations, gasworks and gasometers, new livestock markets and covered markets, schools, churches, football grounds, hospitals and asylums, water pumping stations and sewerage plants totally altered the urban scene, and the country's population tripled with more than seven out of ten people being born in or moving to the towns. The century that followed, leading up to the Millennium's end in 2000, was to be a period of even greater change.

When Queen Victoria died in 1901, she was measured for her coffin by her grandson Kaiser Wilhelm, the London prostitutes put on black mourning and the blinds came down in the villas and terraces spreading out from the old town centres. These centres were reachable by train and tram, by the new bicycles and still newer motor cars, were connected by the new telephone, and lit by gas or even electricity. The shops may have been full of British-made cotton and woollen clothing but the grocers and butchers were selling cheap Danish bacon, Argentinian beef, Australasian mutton and tinned or dried fish and fruit from Canada, California and South Africa. Most of these goods were carried in British-built-and-crewed ships burning Welsh steam coal.

As the first decade moved on, the Open Spaces Act meant more parks, bowling greens and cricket pitches. The First World War transformed the place of women, as they took over many men's jobs. Its other legacies were the war memorials which joined the statues of Victorian worthies in main squares round the land. After 1918 death duties and higher taxation bit hard, and a quarter of England changed hands in the space of only a few years.

The multiple shop – the chain store – appeared in the high street: Sainsburys, Maypole, Lipton's, Home & Colonial, the Fifty Shilling Tailor, Burton, Boots, W.H. Smith. The shopper was spoilt for choice, attracted by the brash fascias and advertising hoardings for national brands like Bovril, Pears Soap, and Ovaltine. Many new buildings began to be seen, such as garages, motor showrooms, picture palaces (cinemas), 'palais de dance', and ribbons of 'semis' stretched along the roads and new bypasses and onto the new estates nudging the green belts.

During the 1920s cars became more reliable and sophisticated as well as commonplace, with developments like the electric self-starter making them easier for women to drive. Who wanted to turn a crank handle in the new short skirt? This was, indeed, the electric age as much as the motor era. Trolley buses, electric trams and trains extended mass transport and electric light replaced gas in the street and the home, which itself was groomed by the vacuum cleaner.

A major jolt to the march onward and upward was administered by the Great Depression of the early 1930s. The older British industries –

textiles, shipbuilding, iron, steel, coal – were already under pressure from foreign competition when this worldwide slump arrived. Luckily there were new diversions to alleviate the misery. The 'talkies' arrived in the cinemas; more and more radios and gramophones were to be found in people's homes; there were new women's magazines, with fashion, cookery tips and problem pages; football pools; the flying feats of women pilots like Amy Johnson; the Loch Ness Monster; cheap chocolate and the drama of Edward VIII's abdication.

Things were looking up again by 1936 and new light industry was booming in the Home Counties as factories struggled to keep up with the demand for radios, radiograms, cars and electronic goods, including the first television sets. The threat from Hitler's Germany meant rearmament, particularly of the airforce, which stimulated aircraft and aero engine firms. If you were lucky and lived in the south, there was good money to be earned. A semi-detached house cost £450, a Morris Cowley £150. People may have smoked like chimneys but life expectancy, since 1918, was up by 15 years while the birth rate had almost halved.

In some ways it is the little memories that seem to linger longest from the Second World War: the kerbs painted white to show up in the

A W.H.Smith shop front in Beaconsfield, 1922.

blackout, the rattle of ack-ack shrapnel on roof tiles, sparrows killed by bomb blast. The biggest damage, apart from London, was in the south-west (Plymouth, Bristol) and the Midlands (Coventry, Birmingham). Postwar reconstruction was rooted in the Beveridge Report which set out the expectations for the Welfare State. This, together with the nationalisation of the Bank of England, coal, gas, electricity and the railways, formed the programme of the Labour government in 1945.

Children collecting aluminium to help the war effort, London, 1940s. (*IWM*)

Times were hard in the late 1940s, with rationing even more stringent than during the war. Yet this was, as has been said, 'an innocent and well-behaved era'. The first let-up came in 1951 with the Festival of Britain and there was another fillip in 1953 from the Coronation, which incidentally gave a huge boost to the spread of TV. By 1954 leisure motoring had been resumed but the Comet – Britain's best hope for taking on the American aviation industry – suffered a series of mysterious crashes. The Suez debacle of 1956 was followed by an acceleration in the withdrawal from Empire, which had begun in 1947 with the Independence of India. Consumerism was truly born with the advent of commercial TV and most homes soon boasted washing machines, fridges, electric irons and fires.

A street party to celebrate the Queen's Coronation, June 1953. (*Hulton Getty Picture Collection*)

The *Lady Chatterley* obscenity trial in 1960 was something of a straw in the wind for what was to follow in that decade. A collective loss of inhibition seemed to sweep the land, as the Beatles and the Rolling Stones transformed popular music, and retailing, cinema and the theatre were revolutionised. Designers, hairdressers, photographers and models moved into places vacated by an Establishment put to flight by the new breed of satirists spawned by *Beyond the Fringe* and *Private Eye*.

In the 1970s Britain seems to have suffered a prolonged hangover after the excesses of the previous decade. Ulster, inflation and union troubles were not made up for by entry into the EEC, North Sea Oil, Women's Lib or, indeed, Punk Rock. Mrs Thatcher applied the corrective in the 1980s, as the country moved more and more from its old manufacturing base over to providing services, consulting, advertising, and expertise in the 'invisible' market of high finance or in IT.

The post-1945 townscape has seen changes to match those in the worlds of work, entertainment and politics. In 1952 the Clean Air Act served notice on smogs and pea-souper fogs, smuts and blackened buildings, forcing people to stop burning coal and go over to smokeless sources of heat and energy. In the same decade some of the best urban building took place in the 'new towns' like Basildon, Crawley, Stevenage and Harlow. Elsewhere open warfare was declared on slums and what was labelled inadequate, cramped, back-to-back, two-up, two-down, housing. The new 'machine for living in' was a flat in a high-rise block. The architects and planners who promoted these were in league with the traffic engineers, determined to keep the motor car moving whatever the price in multi-storey car parks, meters, traffic wardens and ring roads. The old pollutant, coal smoke, was replaced by petrol and diesel exhaust, and traffic noise.

Punk rockers demonstrate their anarchic style during the 1970s. (*Barnaby's Picture Library*)

Fast food was no longer only a pork pie in a pub or fish-and-chips. There were Indian curry houses, Chinese take-aways and American-style hamburgers, while the drinker could get away from beer in a wine bar. Under the impact of television the big Gaumonts and Odeons closed or were rebuilt as multi-screen cinemas, while the palais de dance gave way to discos and clubs.

From the late 1960s the introduction of listed buildings and conservation areas, together with the growth of preservation societies, put a brake on 'comprehensive redevelopment'. The end of the century and the start of the Third Millennium see new challenges to the health of towns and the wellbeing of the nine out of ten people who now live urban lives. The fight is on to prevent town centres from dying, as patterns of housing and shopping change, and edge-of-town supermarkets exercise the attractions of one-stop shopping. But as banks and department stores close, following the haberdashers, greengrocers, butchers and ironmongers, there are signs of new growth such as farmers' markets, and corner stores acting as pick-up points where customers collect shopping ordered on-line from web sites.

Futurologists tell us that we are in stage two of the consumer revolution: a shift from mass consumption to mass customisation driven by a

Millennium celebrations over the Thames at Westminster, New Year's Eve, 1999. (*Barnaby's Picture Library*)

desire to have things that fit us and our particular lifestyle exactly, and for better service. This must offer hope for small city-centre shop premises, as must the continued attraction of physical shopping, browsing and being part of a crowd: in a word, 'shoppertainment'. Another hopeful trend for towns is the growth in the number of young people postponing marriage and looking to live independently, alone, where there is a buzz, in 'swinging single cities'. Theirs is a 'flats-and-cafés' lifestyle, in contrast to the 'family suburbs', and certainly fits in with government's aim of building 60 per cent of the huge amount of new housing needed on 'brown' sites, recycled urban land. There looks to be plenty of life in the British town yet.

Newcastle: An Introduction

The images contained within this book have been carefully selected to reflect Newcastle and its people. Drawing on the private photograph albums of local folk, collectors, keen photographers, and a few images derived from that most unorthodox of professional sources, bric-a-brac fairs, this book provides us with a rich mixture of the people, places and events in Newcastle and looks at how much the heart of 'Geordieland' has altered over the years.

Newcastle West End during the mid-1930s. Children at play in an area which has long been demolished.

The typical definition of a Geordie is someone born on the north side of the Tyne in an area stretching, perhaps, to the coast, Whitley Bay and Tynemouth, although this interpretation of Geordie territory and homeland is often the subject of abundant heated arguments and counter-arguments. For my own part, a Geordie is someone who was born 'up here' and who has the Geordie accent, whether their birth certificate says Newcastle or somewhere 'ten miles out'. The actual Geordie dialect is unique, utilised to full strength in the 1862 song, 'Blaydon Races'.

Only a handful of cities in addition to London have attracted as much interest as Newcastle. Its individualistic streets, winding alleys, pubs, hotels and landmarks are what made Newcastle the city it was and is. Few buildings and landmarks of the distant past survive today, with the exception of, for example, the Castle, Grey's Monument, the familiar image of the Tyne Bridge, and other notable buildings scattered here and there.

Inside Newcastle Central Station in the early 1970s. Porters and commuters mix at a somewhat quiet time of the day.

I have been able to gather together a sequence of impressive, previously unpublished photographs which will no doubt rouse the senses and take older readers back to the time of their youth. The 'younger ones' may be astonished by how Newcastle used to look and can only imagine what it must have been like to walk the streets in such bygone times as the early 1940s when the threat to housing and buildings of prestige was not the bulldozer but the might of German bombing.

The most striking transformations during the twentieth century happened along Newcastle's Quayside, where mass demolition has claimed some of the city's more interesting buildings. The 1960s cleared much of the old housing, forcing Newcastle into a radical conversion. The 1970s brought the Metro train service and Eldon Square, which although a revolutionary shopping experience, also delivered the death knell of some smaller stores that had hitherto managed to survive in the absence of stiff competition.

The Bigg Market (formerly named the Oat Market) is a thriving force, a major attraction today for the young, who are continually drawn from miles around to sample its unrivalled night life. However, 100 years ago, it was a much calmer place, especially at the weekends, devoid of night clubs and bars, although still energetic with trade and the noise of footsteps over cobbles.

The football team, Newcastle United, is known throughout the world for its dedication and talented players, especially key striker Alan Shearer and the current manager Bobby Robson. The Magpies' loyal band of fans has followed the club through good and bad times. Newcastle United's adopted 'son', Kevin Keegan, former player and manager, worked hard in the 1990s to put the club on a positive route to the successful position it occupies in the twenty-first century.

Equally famous is Newcastle Breweries' Brown Ale, or 'Broon Ale', whose aficionados include veteran leading American actor and director Clint Eastwood. The annual BUPA Great North Run also attracts global attention, with world-class athletes, club runners and enthusiastic

The original part of Eldon Square, Newcastle, 1969, well before the shopping complex.

people from all walks of life and of all ages, eager to participate in this thrilling event.

Another exciting aspect of life in Newcastle is that it is attracting the interest of TV programme and film makers who are more than willing to feature the city and its extremities in their small-screen and cinematic projects. This is strengthening Newcastle and making it the 'in' place to be. Who needs Hollywood?

A well-to-do gentleman walks along Heaton Road, c. 1910. This image is part of the postcard on page 23. Curiously, two photographs exist of the same scene, both taken within a split second by different cameras.

The North-East in general has produced a wealth of famous people in years gone by, some of whom weren't even born in the city, but are nevertheless thought of as 'Geordies' (perhaps because of their accents), celebrities who typify Newcastle and who have been proud to wear their 'Geordie pride', such as football legends Jack and Sir Bobby Charlton, the late novelist Dame Catherine Cookson, rock singer and songwriter Sting, actor and singer Jimmy Nail, actress Denise Welch, and inventor-engineer George Stephenson. These people, the TV and movie productions, and business entrepreneurs like Sir John Hall and Karl Watkin have all gained widespread recognition, putting the city on national and global maps, and overturning the misguided opinion, often held by southerners, that Newcastle is still a place of 'flat caps and whippets'!

The Theatre Royal, People's Theatre and City Hall continue to this day to provide the ultimate in live entertainment, making Newcastle a bedrock of arts and music. A world-first, The International Centre for LIFE, is a £70 million complex housed on a 10-acre site. There is no other centre which brings research, medical and commercial applications, ethics, education and entertainment relating to DNA together under one roof. The International Centre for LIFE incorporates LIFE Interactive World, the Bioscience Centre, LIFELAB, LIFE Conference and Banqueting, and The Institute of Human Genetics and PEALS. There is no question about it: the city of Newcastle has much to look forward to in the years ahead.

The compilation of this book was an arduous task, but also a very enjoyable experience. The availability of so many excellent pictures did not in itself make this book. In order to give an overall feel of Newcastle in the last 100 years, I had to employ a certain degree of ruthlessness in my choice of photographs. Cutting back on the number of images was regrettable but necessary, or this work could have run into several volumes. While the bulk of the book focuses on the centre of Newcastle, I decided it was worth venturing out further afield to places like Gosforth Park racecourse, The Three Mile Inn pub, and Heaton Road; I have done this because Newcastle in a sense extends beyond its centre and I thought it would be interesting to show some of the places frequented by ordinary folk out for entertainment or a drink.

Earlier, I mentioned that some of the photographs in this book were discovered in among bric-a-brac: this included publicity shots of actors who used to tread the boards before the First World War (see pages 23–7). These pictures – all of them signed – are terrific examples of the kind of photographic material of historical and regional importance that is out there, just waiting to be discovered. Credit must also be given to brothers Edmund and Harold Atkinson, whose

The Northumberland Arms Pub, which was later renamed Rosie's, on Stowell Street, 1971.

Filming Dame Catherine Cookson's *The Fifteen Streets*, late 1980s. Dame Catherine produced books at a tremendous speed yet their quality never suffered – romantic, but gritty. A TV production note: the cobbles seen in this picture are rubber mats!

personal photographic collection reaches back near seventy years: over 100 of their photographs appear in the following pages. So, if this book teaches you anything, it is that you must think twice before discarding old photographs. You may be throwing away a part of our local history, something which once destroyed can never be replaced.

One final point. Aside from the heritage, the famous, the important, the buildings, the architecture and the landmarks, we must remember the 'ordinary Newcastle people', warm, trusting and affable, who make this city glorious. No matter where you travel, you'll always find the friendly face of a Geordie!

John Alexander, 2000

The New Century Unfolds

The early part of the twentieth century, and a young boy poses for his photograph at the Leighton Studios, which was situated at 12 Northumberland Street, Newcastle. It is clear that the boy and his family were not working class.

A pre-First World War Newcastle wedding raises few laughs as the bride and groom stand with a lone bridesmaid and elderly relatives in a photograph taken in a back garden. Their apparent 'gloominess' can be explained. During that period, cameras had very long exposures. The person getting photographed had two choices. Wear a fixed grin, or look impassive.

Neville Street, Westgate Road and Stephenson Monument, *c.* 1905. To the left is the old Douglas Hotel. The then familiar tram lines are clearly visible.

A fascinating glimpse of Newcastle's ancient Grey Friars Monastery, in a sketch drawn around 1900.

Grainger Street, *c.* 1912. The spectacular vision of the 700-year-old St John's Church is to the right. And take a look at the Victorian lamppost.

Stephenson's Monument and St John's Church, Newcastle, *c.* 1919. The monument was erected in 1862.

The Newcastle Central Station as it looked nearly 100 years ago. The Royal Station Hotel is to the left.

Heaton Road, Newcastle, in the Edwardian age, *c.* 1915. The old cobbled road is a complete contrast to the present-day tarmac (see page 16).

Actors such as G. Featherstone were numerous in Newcastle before the First World War. This publicity photograph was taken in 1910 and belongs to a very rare collection, recently discovered. The following pages feature other local thespians who used to tread the boards in the Newcastle of old.

Local actor E.G. Macdonald dons military attire in a production of *The Pirates*, 1914. The following photographs show actors in a variety of different roles and costumes.

This actress's name is unknown but she is pictured here playing Lady Harlington in a production of *The Young Lieutenant*, 1911. The set consists of a ship, supposedly docked on the Tyne.

This is another thespian, whose stage name was Quintin Golder. It may have also been his real name, but that is highly unlikely. This picture was taken around 1911. Golder acted in Newcastle but lived for a short time in South Shields.

G. Featherstone was a master of disguise. Here he is in 1910, looking a lot like Robin Hood! Actors in those days went to great lengths to make their roles appear real. Wearing well-tailored costumes and theatrical make-up was essential.

A Newcastle company, consisting of females only, gather together for a rousing musical performed in the city in 1912. Among them is a lady called Norah Elliot.

G. Featherstone is at it again, 1908. This time he's dressed in some sort of Mexican garb, with rifle in hand.

G. Featherstone, seen here in 1909. And, yes, the moustache is false. The tree would have been real though.

Elliot G. Macdonald dons a clown's black-and-white attire, with collar and hat, for a production entitled, *La Gigalo*, 1910. Macdonald played a character called Vincent. The show was staged at the Tyne Theatre.

Elliot G. Macdonald in the Mikado, 1914. He wrote New Year wishes to a friend on the back of this postcard.

Another cast member of *La Gigalo*, 1910. Credit must be given to the costume designers who really knew their trade. The quality was superb.

Will Wairson who had a minor role in the *La Gigalo*, 1910.

Agnes Davidson often played the part of 'the lady of the manor', which was partly down to her aristocratic appearance.

G. Featherstone once played the central role of the Dandy in a local theatre production staged during the mid-1920s. He is seen here in the original costume drama version from 1910.

P. Fairclough Photographics was situated on 30 Scotswood Road, opposite the then Cattle Market, Newcastle. This girl is pictured holding a bucket and fishing net, props that were supplied to make the photograph more interesting.

Inside the Central Station, *c.* 1912. This area would be far busier today. Of course, everything is computerised in the year 2000. In the old days, communication with passengers and other stations was very basic, yet still reliable.

Inside the Central Station, *c.* 1919. To the right there are a row of waiting rooms – ladies and gentlemen were expected to remain separate – lavatories and wash rooms.

An army fellow, photographed *c.* 1916. The chap's identity is unknown. Nevertheless it is a fine portrait of a brave man prepared to die for his country.

Back home from the Great War, Jesmond, *c.* 1919. The horrors of war affected many men's state of mind. This officer is clearly delighted to be home with his family and friends.

During the First World War, most men believed its intensity and the number of lives lost meant that they might be next in line to die. Weddings were quickly arranged during 'leave', just in case the men were not reunited with their sweethearts again. This Newcastle photograph from 1916 features an upper-class officer and his bride, together with family and friends.

Soldiers pose at F. Macfadyen's Photographics, 151 Barras Bridge, Newcastle upon Tyne, *c.* 1916. Note the man, in the middle of the first row, who appears to have a false right hand. If this were the case, it was no doubt an amputation sustained during front-line action. He would henceforth have taken an administrative role in the war.

Northumberland Street, *c.* 1920. Complete with trams, horses and carts, this delightful scene would soon disappear with the advent of the motor car which was becoming more available and less expensive to purchase.

Newcastle Central Station, *c.* 1919. The mass of train lines is testimony to the fact that this was then the largest railway crossing in the world.

Hopes, Dreams and Reality

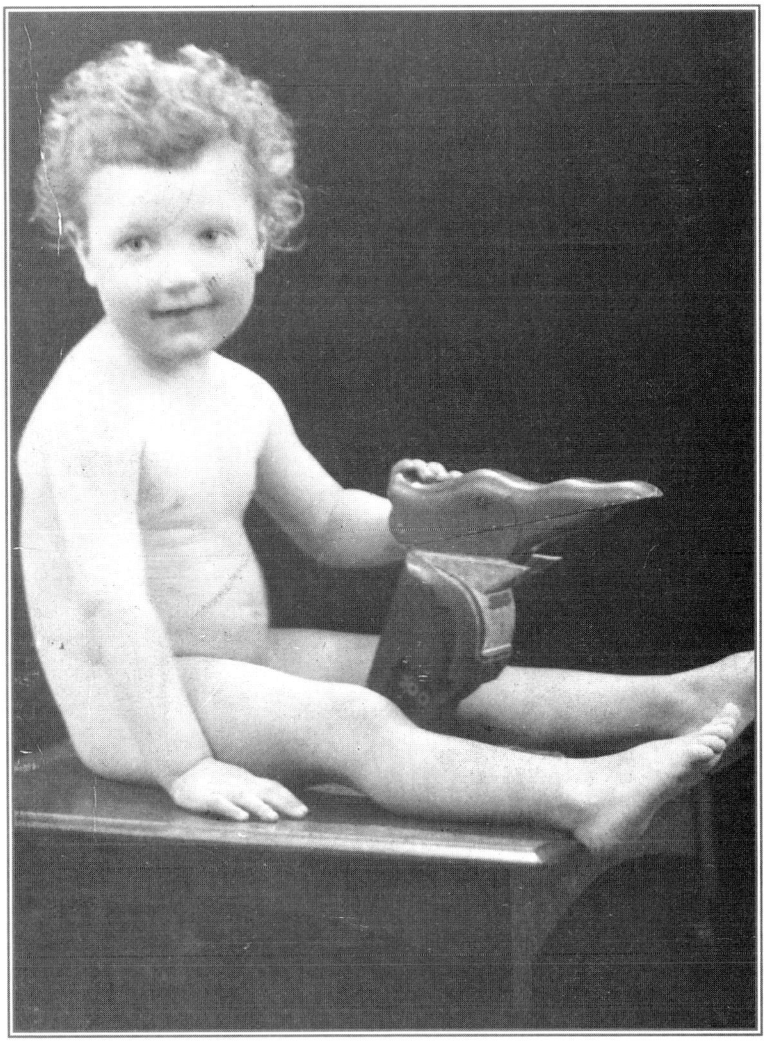

This two-year-old boy is Grenrick Carrick, winner of the *Daily Sketch* newspaper's healthy babies contest, *c.* 1932. A fine mop of hair, but was he a little too flabby around the waist to be really worthy of the title?

Looking up Grey Street to the Grey's Monument, *c.* 1927. To the left is The Royal Turks Head Hotel, with the Theatre Royal to the right. The presence of motor cars was beginning to be felt on the streets of Newcastle.

Black Gate and Castle, *c.* 1921. Around this time, Newcastle was becoming a fairly busy city, with the daily influx of cars and trams. Tobacconists and wine and spirit outlets, such as the one seen in the picture, saw their trade boosted.

An aerial shot of St Nicholas Cathedral as seen from the top of the Castle, *c.* 1926, reveals the extent to which the passing of time has brought changes to the city.

Blackett Street in 1925. In view are Barry Noble's Fruiterers and Reed's Clock.

All the hustle and bustle of Northumberland Street, as a policeman directs the traffic, *c.* 1928. To the right is the Pearl Assurance Company.

The Royal Victoria Infirmary in 1929, twenty years before the introduction of the National Health Service.

The grand opening ceremony of the Tyne Bridge by His Majesty King George V, 10 October 1928. The occasion was also attended by VIPs and the members of the church.

Tyne Bridge, *c.* 1928. This classic view shows boats and ships of old on the River Tyne, running under all four bridges.

The Renwick Memorial to the lost souls of the First World War, *c.* 1928. The monument is an impressive and fitting tribute to the men who fought and died for Great Britain. St Thomas' Church is in the background.

An historical pageant took place in Leazes Park in 1932. It proved to be a great day out for friends and family – luckily there was a photographer present to capture the event.

Two local residents have a laugh at the same historical pageant seen at the bottom of the previous page. And you can just imagine what the finely dressed man is saying to this woman: 'Well, hello, my lady! Pray may I introduce myself?'

A visit to a Newcastle photographer, on 17 Saltwell Road, in December 1939, provides this festive, family snap of two children, who are most probably brothers. The book the smaller child is holding is a tot's *Tales for Tinies* ABC.

The Tyne Bridge on a sleepy Sunday morning, late 1930s. You will never see this sight again – only two cars travelling along it and no congestion.

Left: Vehicles line up along Dean Street, *c*. 1930. It is possible that there may have been an important function taking place nearby. This view is supported when one considers the number of hotels and pubs in the vicinity.

Newcastle has produced many historical pageants. This one took place sometime in the late 1930s, with the Honorary Secretary Mrs S.R. Vereker making an appearance, dressed in an attractive costume.

The Nettleton children relax in the bright summer sunshine of August 1939. They are, left to right: Eva, Amy (standing), Frankie (seated), and Rose. Their father John, the author's grandad, can be seen in the shadowed doorway. The outbreak of the Second World War was not far off. For safety, many children were evacuated to the countryside where German bombing was rare. These children were not evacuated, but stayed with their parents instead. They all survived the war.

View of Newcastle and the Tyne Bridge as seen from Bottle Bank, Gateshead, 19 August 1937. In view is St Nicholas Cathedral.

It's difficult to place the exact location of the photograph, although it is Newcastle and was most probably Bull Park. The picture dates from around 1948, and shows Royal Air Force personnel proudly sitting next to what looks like a Mustang.

Workers have a laugh together, standing next to one of Tower's Brown Ale delivery trucks, Newcastle, 1946. Tower was a small company, in competition with the original 'Broon Ale'.

The Three Mill Inn, 1949. The couple in the middle are John and Eva Alexander with Amy Nettleton to the left.

Newcastle has produced some major sporting stars, including Alan Shearer, Peter Beardsley, Jackie Milburn, Brendan Foster and Steve Cram. These two chaps look all set for a day at the track, *c.* 1946.

Turners at Camera House, Pink Lane, consisted of five floors catering for all photography requirements. This advertisement is from 1948. Turners later merged with another company and changed name.

The Brush Factory, Newcastle, 1947. Making brushes was a difficult and messy task. First the brush hairs were gathered together then dipped into a tar-like substance. The handle was then attached. The female employees here had to wear special clothing and gloves to avoid the burning sensation caused by the liquid material if it came into contact with the skin.

A weekday afternoon in the vicinity of the Quayside, Sandhill, late 1940s. There is a noticeable lack of pedestrians for the time of day. The large building to the left is the Guildhall.

Robson's Furniture Store at Spital Tongues, Newcastle, summer 1948. Workers and their families prepare for a day out to Bamburgh and Seahouses. Typically, it was raining, which put a dampener on the occasion. Roland Cooper is second from the right, with his pal Jimmy Brown on his left. Robson's had shops on Northumberland Street and Saville Row.

Three factory workers relax is the summer sunshine, *c.* 1947. They were most likely administrative staff, perhaps typists.

NORMAN

Gosforth Park Races, Newcastle, 6 June 1948. This fascinating photograph makes one feel that one is there watching the horses fly past the winning post. Who'd have thought the backs of people's heads could be so interesting!?

Mrs D.R. Durrant on her wedding day during the late 1940s. Mrs Durrant was a keen ballroom dancer in her youth. She and her partner won various competitions.

HMS *Tyne*, docked at Newcastle Quayside *c*. 1949. The *Tyne* had a fine history of service dating back to the Second World War.

The '50s

Fire in Northumberland Street on a Sunday morning, 1957. Out of view are a sizeable number of people watching the firemen fight the blaze from a cordoned-off area where the cameraman is also standing.

A typical 'Geordie bloke' puffs on his pipe with his pet dog keeping him company, *c.* 1951. Such real-life characters inspired the popular *Daily Mirror* newspaper strip, Andy Capp.

Taking a 'bogey' ride in Sandyford, Mary Naple Street, 1960. The lady is Meg Colpitts. She is seen holding her young child. The other children lived in the street.

Newcastle Boy Scouts have an activity weekend in Gosforth Park, *c.* 1958. These weekends were held regularly and were extremely popular with the children. Note the presence of the vicar in the white jacket and the cooks seated at either end of the group.

Summertime and these children are celebrating something special during 1956. Most probably it's a kiddies' birthday party. Hence the hats. They are clearly enjoying themselves as they wave their toy axes.

Newcastle folk enjoying the summer weather in a day out to some unknown holiday destination, mid-1950s. Trips were usually to places like the Lakes and Edinburgh. The Priory Motor Coach Company Limited was formed in 1929 as a home business in Waterloo Place, North Shields. Its founder, George Chapman, died in 1955, but the company continued to flourish and grow. It is presently based in Church Way, North Shields.

A wedding in the 1950s. This couple's families have obviously spared no expense in making their special day highly memorable.

The Side, where it joins Dean Street, early 1950s. To the left is Milburn House, built in 1905. It was once the largest office spaces in the country. Note that the building opposite was being shored up at the time. The cobbles have recently been covered.

This building on the outskirts of Byker must have been a strong contender for the 'thinnest' house in Britain. Alas, this abode has long since gone and, by mid-century, the word 'demolish' was starting to come into the Newcastle vocabulary.

A tramcar derailment on the junction of St Nicholas Street and Westgate Road in Newcastle, *c.* 1952. The bystander to the right obviously finds the whole incident interesting. Tram guards are trying to straighten out the situation. Does anyone remember Albatross Flour?

ALBATROSS

Another view of the tram car derailment seen on the previous page. Passengers wait patiently for the tram to get moving while drivers and conductors chat away.

This magnificent picture is a striking image of Newcastle in 1952, with tram cars seen on St Nicholas Street. Small crowds gathered to witness what transpired.

Grey Street, *c.* 1954. Visible are Lloyds Bank and Mawson, Swan & Morgan, which is now Waterstone's bookshop. Most people appear to be smartly dressed in Newcastle in the 1950s – suits for the men and well-presented frocks for the ladies. No jeans, T-shirts, track suits or trainers!

Actor James Hayter made an appearance at the Theatre Royal in the early 1950s, and presented one fan with this charming photograph. James Hayter starred in an array of British comedy movies, before finding TV fame in *Are You Being Served?* in the late 1970s, playing the character Mr Tebbs. Hayter is probably best known, though, as the voice behind the TV commercial for Mr Kipling's Cakes!

A Pacific-class streamlined engine, arriving at the Central Station, *c.* 1958.

On the corner of the Cloth Market and Mosley Street, *c.* 1958. The statue of Queen Victoria is on the right.

Grainger Street, 1956. Harker's Furniture Store appears to be attracting potential customers who are doing a bit of window shopping. To the left of the picture two women and a young boy wait for a bus.

The corner of Westgate Road and Grainger Street, 1956. Officer workers arrive ready for the 9 to 5 shift. While they are working, shoppers fill the streets.

Grainger Street, *c.* 1959. Shoppers are in the city visiting the many and varied outlets.

'Ho! Ho! Ho!' Santa's Grotto at Fenwick's Store, Northumberland Street in the mid-1950s. Fenwick's has long made Christmas special for children and adults alike. Its famous animated festive window scenes are extremely popular.

Into the Swinging '60s

Jefferson Street, Newcastle. This corner shop was a typical community meeting point. This is just like a scene from Ronnie Barker's *Open All Hours* TV show.

The old Forth Goods Station, Newcastle, *c.* 1960. It has now been demolished and the tracks have been removed.

With bands such as The Beatles making their distinctive mark on the music business, Newcastle seized its opportunity to get in on the scene. The Animals were undoubtedly the most popular of the North-East '60s groups. Not all of the bands became famous, but that didn't stop people trying to get a hit in the 'hit parade', such as this drummer at an audition in 1963.

Newgate Street, 1966. Student rag week has taken over the city. The placard on the Federation Brewery truck is a little near the knuckle even for those days!

Rag week, 1967, on the corner of Grainger Street. The scantily clad ladies dance on what must be quite a chilly day when you consider that the spectators have their coats on.

Hamilton Street, now demolished, in the late 1960s. There is a noticeable lack of people.

Newcastle children at play, *c.* 1964. Even in today's age of computers and expensive toys, children still find immense pleasure in riding a bike and playing with a toy car.

S. Green was a tailor whose shop was situated in Elswick Road, Newcastle. It is seen here in 1969. A rather unusual selling point for the business was the advertisement in the window advising customers that it was possible for 'gents' suits' to be made into 'ladies' costumes' – in addition to the more familiar tailoring services.

The Grainger and Percy Building Society on Hood Street in 1969. Next door is the Tyne Hotel.

Newcastle city centre, 1967.

Stanhope Street, in the late 1960s. Structurally, there was nothing wrong with these houses but, like a lot of old housing, modern building plans took priority and they were demolished.

Exhibition Park, 1968. This rocket was a fascinating attraction at the fair. The RAF's Red Arrows also made an appearance on the same afternoon.

How it used to be: old Eldon Square, October 1969. A serene place to read a newspaper and even have a nap on a summer's day.

A typical '60s scene. A mother and her daughter, the bride, chat with a bridesmaid before the wedding. The bride's glasses are a real giveaway of the period.

A weekday afternoon outside Newcastle Central station on Neville Street, 1969.

Left: Late '60s 'flower power' strikes Newcastle, with a local girl all togged out for a 'hippies' music event on the town moor. Do you recognise yourself in the crowd? Or maybe you're the girl with the headband.

Right: The 'groovy' 1960s saw the birth of outdoor music concerts and hippy weekends, illustrated by this picture from 1968. Teenagers had a new-found freedom. Britain had come a long way in just fifteen years from the well-presented young person in collar and tie, or long skirts, and a nice hairdo, to outlandish cheese-cloth shirts, flesh-revealing clothes, drugs and free-flowing alcohol.

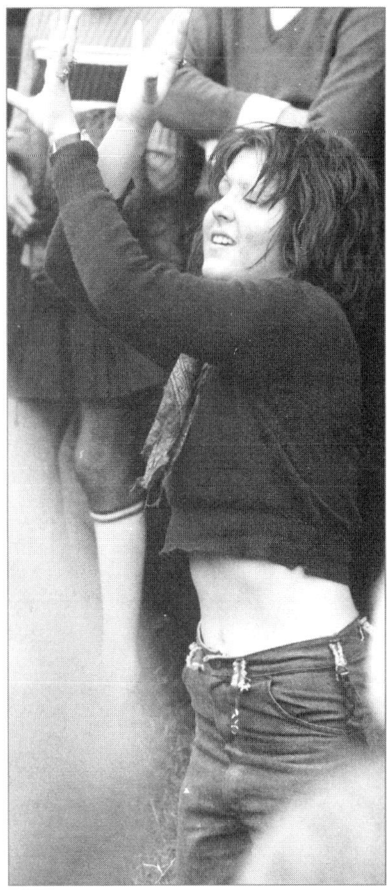

Catching a train in Newcastle via the Riverside line in 1969 meant walking through the gates at the Central Station. There porters were on hand to check tickets.

The late, lamented Chain Bridge, 1966. Shortly after this photograph was taken, the bridge was destroyed.

Remember Gallowgate Baths? This outstanding Victorian structure with a very interesting façade is seen here in 1969. Sadly, it has now been demolished.

Having a smoke in the centre of Newcastle. The '60s clothing is certainly something for connoisseurs of fashion. This was the attire that Twiggy, the top female model of the period, was showing off on the catwalks of Britain. Twiggy's almost pop-star status and influence on fashion were dazzling. All the young '60s girls wanted to be thin, just like her. Twiggy's incredibly svelte figure introduced a new phrase into common speech: 'I've seen more fat on a chip.'

This magazine advertisement from 1966 presents the opening of a new restaurant on the corner of Gallowgate and Percy Street. The theme of football is never far away in Newcastle, as the reference to the Magpies clearly demonstrates.

Changes, Scooters and Flares

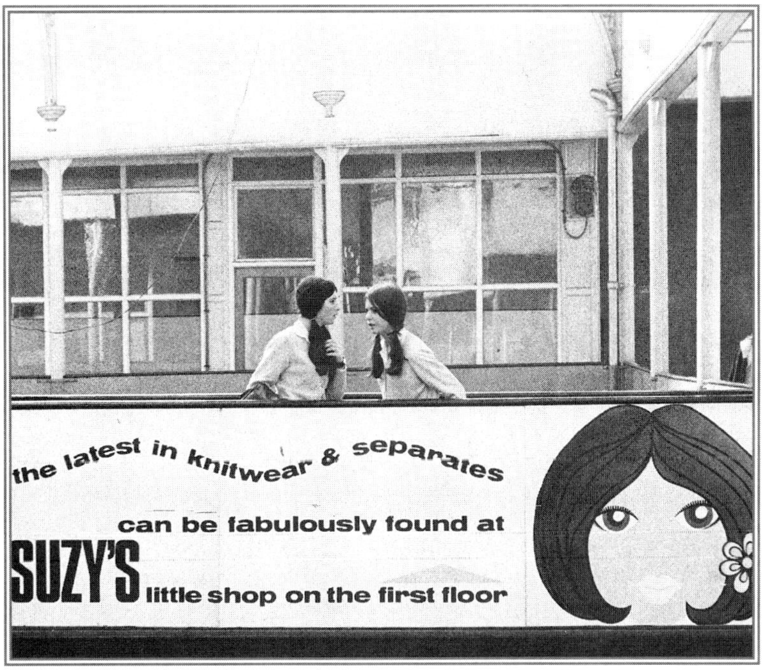

Two teenage girls with their hair in bunches chat outside Suzy's 'little shop on the first floor' in the centre of Newcastle. The pictures in this chapter include snaps from the 1970s and trace developments in Newcastle right through to the 1980s.

OLD GOLD. SILVER. COINS.
WAR MEDALS. PISTOLS Etc.
BRASS. COPPER. BOUGHT
H. Krolick
ANTIQUES.
BROAD CHARE
QUAYSIDE CAFE

Broad Chare, 1970. An old pawn shop requests old silver coins, war medals and pistols. Next to it is the Quayside Café, with a 'Beech Nut' chewing gum machine fixed beside the door. And finally, the Baltic Tavern. Much of what is seen here has now been demolished or renovated.

In the vicinity of Newcastle Central Station, 1971. On this plot of land stood the old cattle market and P. Fairclough Photographics. The actual cattle market itself operated for many decades. It consisted of a large number of pens and above the entrance was the image of a bull's head.

Ye Olde Friars Antique Shoppe was suitably situated in Low Friars Street and is pictured here in 1973. The proprietor J.W. Teare sold everything from curios, silver and pewter to watches and pistols. There were actually two shops owned by J.W. Teare – the other was next door!

A favourite watering hole, The Tyne pub, Quayside, Sandhill corner, 1 January 1970. Here we see The Tyne at the end of its life, closed and boarded up. It had occupied a fine building.

Neville Street, 1970. Once again, the staggering and unique architecture of Newcastle is apparent.

The Tyne Bridge in all its glory, seen from the Quayside, 1 January 1970. There is a large crane to the left of the picture.

Friars Street, 1971. A road sweeper pushes his dustcart up the steep hill, a lone figure, except for all those pigeons.

A Sunday morning, 1972. Market stall-holders set up for business on the Newcastle Quayside under the magnificent Tyne Bridge. This is an old and well-established tradition.

Waterloo Street on a quiet Sunday morning in April 1970. This picture was taken at 7.30 a.m., and the city had yet to wake up.

TELEPHONE

Newcastle Quayside, April 1970. To the left, crowds gather at the weekend stalls and to the right is the old post office and savings bank at Mercantile Chambers. Straight ahead, the King Street sign is visible with a blast from the past – a red telephone box. The lady and gentleman in the foreground have found something interesting to stare at but it can't be as intriguing as why the lady has a parrot perched on her right hand.

Flared trousers, outrageous pullovers, loud skirts, medallions, Jason King moustaches and bad haircuts meet when friends gather in a Bigg Market pub for a drink, mid-1970s. And has anyone told the ventriloquist's dummy it's his turn to get a round in?

The Bigg Market, 1970. A regular haunt among the young who are drawn to taste the city's unrivalled nightlife. The Rutherford Memorial Fountain, which dates back to 1894, is in view.

Newcastle Quayside, 1970. Cail & Sons Limited, Printers and Stationers, was established in 1830. This shop was closing for business when this picture was taken. Long ago, many outlets thrived on the Quayside but when some traders began to move further into the city, others lost out and were forced to close.

Exhibition Park (Bull Park), North Road, Newcastle, 1972. All this has since gone, as road widening claimed the entrance and the row of trees, which made way for a new motorway.

Grey Street, 1973. The Monument was erected in memory of the Earl Grey of Howick. The column, 135 feet tall and with 164 internal steps, is a mighty landmark, reviving memories of the past. The scooters parked at the side of the road were a 'must have' for young people in the 1970s.

Actor James Bolan on location with fellow actors and extras in Newcastle for the making of the hit 1970s TV drama, *When the Boat Comes In*. The series ran from 1976 to 1981 (with breaks) and gave Bolan the opportunity to shake free of his comedy role in *Whatever Happened to the Likely Lads?* Born in Sunderland, but an adopted Geordie, Bolan returned to his northern roots with a one-off series, *Andy Capp*, broadcast on television in 1988.

Blackfriars before the restoration. A road sweeper with an old dustcart.

This is the massive Newcastle Warehouse Company Limited, Sandhill, 1971. It was no longer occupied when the photograph was taken.

The end of the old Redhaugh Bridge, 1974. This hut has been demolished.

NEWCASTLE
RIVERSIDE
A3

July 1973 and the Riverside line is on the brink of being closed. This area at Newcastle Central Station was closed off and the tracks were filled in, leaving the original platforms and the flattened-out surface which was later used as a car park.

Inside the Central Station, 1974. This area was demolished to make way for yet another car park. The poster advertisements include one for John Gibson's popular sporting column in the *Evening Chronicle*.

Exhibition Park, 1973. Only one boat is afloat, being rowed across the lake in fine summer weather.

An elderly gentleman with a stick walks from the bottom of Brighton Grove across Nun's Moor Park, 1973.

Summer, 1970. La Dolce Vita was situated in Low Friar Street, a regular haunt for Newcastle folk, such as these two young men pictured out for a good evening's entertainment. La Dolce Vita attracted some major '60s stars, including Val Doonican, and even children's favourites Terry Hall and Lenny the Lion!

The Rutherford Memorial drinking fountain in the Bigg Market, mid-1970s.

Construction of the Metro Bridge during the late 1970s. The Tyne and Wear Metro system is run by Nexus.

The famous Scotswood Road, as mentioned in the 1862 song 'Blaydon Races'. The boarded-up pub and graffiti were an unfortunate sight in the early 1970s.

The Closing Century

Peter Davison and Robert Glenister in Newcastle in 1981 for the filming of the BBC comedy show *Sink or Swim*. The series was mainly set in London, but Davison and Glenister had one scene in the North-East. Davison played the older brother, Brian. The show ran from 1980 to 1982. Increasingly, TV programme and movie-makers are heading for the North-East, especially Newcastle. The movie that set the ball rolling was *Payroll*, made in the early 1960s and filmed entirely in Tynemouth and Newcastle. The next major picture was the memorable *Get Carter*, starring Michael Caine. Other productions include Sting's *Stormy Monday*, along with television material ranging from Catherine Cookson epics to *Spender* and *Our Friends in the North*. Alas, not all new North-East productions have been successful: in the late 1990s *Quayside*, Tyne Tees Television's soap opera, sank without trace.

Blackfriars, Newcastle, August 1983. After building workers discovered bones, an excavation soon got under way to find out more about who had been buried there and the age of the remains. There was no murder mystery: they were cattle bones.

Soccer legend George Best on location shooting a scene for the children's TV show *SuperGran*, February 1984. George's visit was fleeting. He arrived in the North-East by plane, from London. He acted his part and returned home within hours. Next to George is entertainer Sid Kerr. The chap in the middle is a member of the TV crew.

Blackfriars Place, Newcastle, March 1981. These fine properties are supreme examples of the old architecture in Newcastle. To the left, there is a plaque outside the former residence of engineer Robert Stephenson (1803–59). The plaque informs passers-by that Stephenson 'lived here from his marriage in 1829 until he moved to London in 1833'. During this time he designed and constructed the *Rocket* and later the *Planet*, the prototype for more than a century of steam locomotive development.

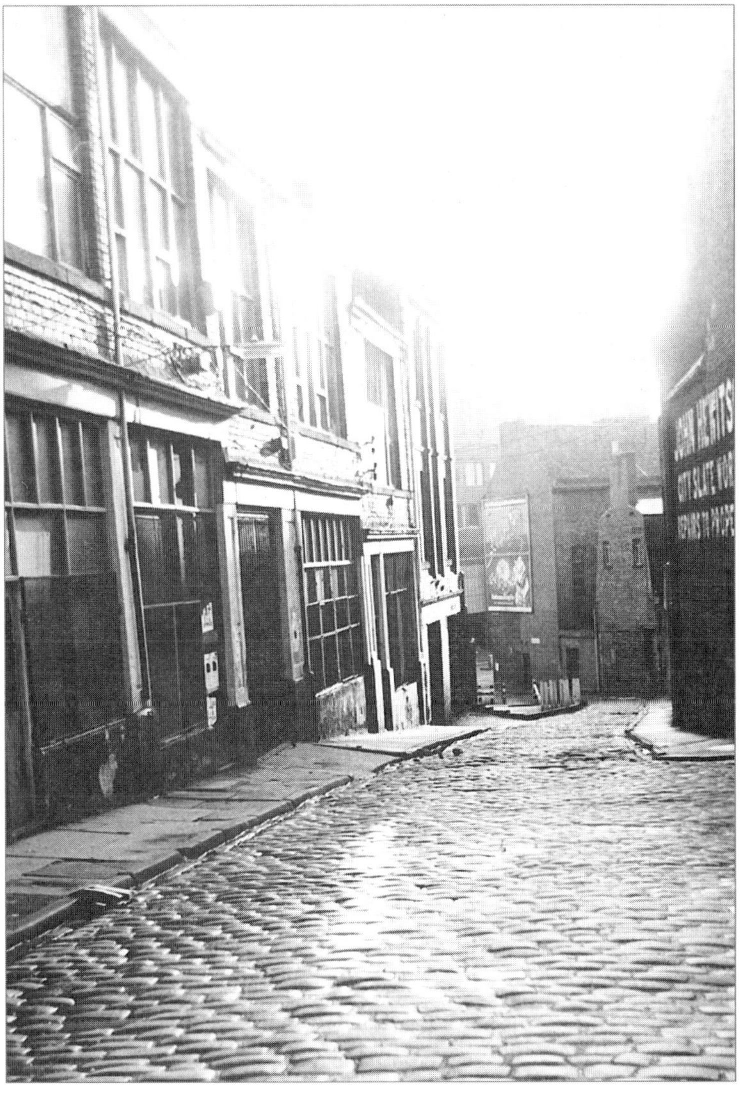

The cobbled, winding alley behind Bath Terrace, 1980. No doubt these were the very same cobbles that Robert Stephenson trod in the mid-nineteenth century.

Two men depart the Telegraph Pub, on the corner of Forth Street and Orchards Street, 1987.

Bath Lane, the entrance to Dennhofer Wines Ltd, 1987.

A throng of shoppers and visitors to the city of Newcastle mingle around Grey's Monument, 1987. The building behind the Monument and to the left used to be a post office but has made way for Monument Mall. Part of the façade to the right has been preserved.

The old Haymarket Hotel, in Percy Street in 1982, before the introduction of the new-style BT telephone boxes.

Newcastle, 1987, Corner Tower, Croft Stairs. This building is centuries old but is curiously still an important part of the twenty-first-century city.

Rutherford Street, Gallagar's Tobacco Factory, 1992, now demolished. The statue of the old dog sat on the top of the building.

Left: The traditional Old George Pub, early 1990s. The Old George is easily one of the finest pubs in the region, in terms of history and charm.

In all their glory – High Level Bridge, Swing Bridge and Tyne Bridge, early 1990s.

Actor Jimmy Nail plays out a scene on location at Newcastle Central Station in September 1992. The *Spender* series gave Jimmy the opportunity to act the part of a tough guy with a heart of gold.

'Roll Cameras. Action!' The Central Station once again, 1992. Local lad Jimmy Nail found fame in the early 1980s playing Oz, the loud-mouthed 'brickie' in *Auf Wiedersehen, Pet*. He later carved out a career as a singer, songwriter, scriptwriter and TV producer.

Chatting to production staff. Jimmy silenced his critics by storming the music charts with hits like 'Love Don't Live Here Anymore', 'Ain't No Doubt', 'Crocodile Shoes' and 'The River', as well as three successful television series. His movie career has included working with Madonna in *Evita*.

Watch them go! Try spotting a familiar face of a relative or friend in this superb shot of the start of the BUPA Great North Run, again taken during the late 1990s.

Around the four-mile mark, the mass of runners are starting to thin out, as the serious runners take control of the race. Water stations are at hand along the course to stop the participants dehydrating.

The BUPA Great North Run is renowned for producing gritty participants, such as this disabled man who completed the 13 miles with unbounded determination.

The annual BUPA Great North Run attracts global attention with world-class athletes, club runners and enthusiastic people from all walks of life and of all ages, eager to participate in this thrilling event. This is a close-up view of the lead runners in a race during the later 1990s.

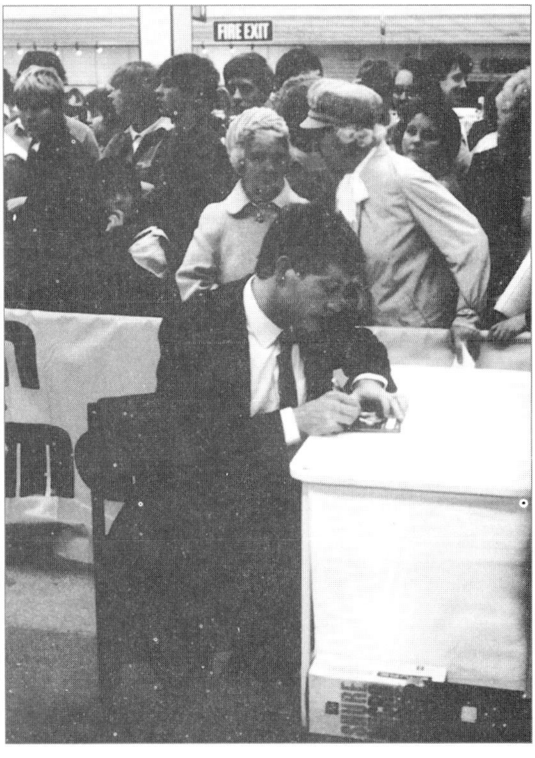

Then World Snooker Champion Steve Davis signing autographs in Eldon Square, early 1980s. Steve made snooker into a young man's sport after decades of it being dubbed an 'old gentleman's game'. Steve's fans ranged from tots to pensioners, who obviously included these two elderly ladies in the centre of the picture.

St Nicholas Street, 1994. Note the shop called Snoozers – the perfect sleep inducer.

Pilgrim Street, 1994. Northern Goldsmiths has since changed its name to simply Goldsmiths.

Looking down the Tyne, as the Tall Ships gather, 1993. The Cutty Sark Tall Ships Races are named after their sponsor, Cutty Sark Scotch Whisky which, in turn, is named after the nineteenth-century Scottish clipper moored at Greenwich. Cutty Sark Whisky has sponsored the event since 1972, making this the world's longest running sports sponsorship.

The Tall Ships brought the people of the North-East out in their droves, and with sights as spectacular as this wonderful vessel, who could blame them? The Cutty Sark trophy is awarded for promoting international friendship and understanding. The main aims of the event, apart from providing a splendid display of the world's finest ships, are to provide challenge, adventure, commitment, teamwork and thrills.

The true beauty of the ships' splendid design is fully appreciated here. Just think of the work and dedication it must have taken to build these vessels. Between fifteen and thirty nations participate in the Cutty Sark Races each year.

Many of the ships have been crewed by young people between the ages of sixteen and twenty-five. In the race's 25-year history, more than 150,000 young people from around the world have taken part. When the event was last screened on TV, it notched up an amazing 500 million viewers from all over the world.

Bottom of Dean Street, 1994. Rock star Sting's movie *Stormy Monday* was shot around this area some seven years earlier. It scored only minor success at the box office.

A case of the old saluting the new – the Newcastle Monument Mall, late 1990s. A picture of local hero footballer Jackie Milburn can be seen in the window. The area below the 'old' clock and the piper, so rumour has it, was a meeting place for courting couples.

Two students from Newcastle University pose outside the Guildhall in this unusual snapshot taken in 1993. The Guildhall has been in the city for well over 100 years.

Bentick Crescent, Elswick Road, June 1998, at the height of the World Cup. These men erected their own 'bar' in a front garden. As well as being stocked up with crates of beer, pictures of the teams adorn the walls.

TV and radio personality James Whale started his broadcasting career at Metro Radio (later renamed Metro FM) in 1974. His inventive 'Night Owls' show was a revolution in radio; listening figures soared, making both the show and the host a cult figure. James quit the station in the early 1980s to concentrate on TV projects. He made a brief return to Newcastle in November 1997 to present his popular Talk Radio programme. James is pictured here 'off guard', in the company of his PA, enjoying a meal at Sabatini's Restaurant, King Street. Later that night he broadcast his show from the Newcastle *Evening Chronicle* offices in Groat Market.

Looking to the Future

The final chapter of this book is dedicated to Newcastle in the twenty-first century, now that we are into the new Millennium. A lot has transpired in the last 1,000 years, especially in Newcastle's last century. So, as author, I thought that having viewed so much of the past in previous chapters, it would be interesting to concentrate on how Newcastle is today and the bright future that lays ahead. Of course, the following pictures will indeed become part of history one day, and will no doubt provoke abundant curiosity in the people of the future who read this book. Playing her part in this bright new future was Carol Vorderman, pictured above, posing for cameras, having just cut the ribbon to open officially LIFE Interative World. The complex is situated in Times Square. LIFE Interative World, a £25 million state-of the art visitor attraction, opened in Newcastle upon Tyne on 27 May 2000.

TV celebrity Carol Vorderman enjoying the spinning Vortex at LIFE Interactive World, part of The International Centre for LIFE, 2000. Carol opened the centre free of charge.

LIFE Interactive World's Crazy Motion Ride is an exhilarating experience that all the family can enjoy – if you are prepared for a rip-roaring ride.

It's a dummies' 'LIFE' at Interactive World's Tunnel of Love. This beer never goes flat. Eccentric exhibits such as this have sent Interactive World's takings soaring, making this one of the most popular attractions in the North-East.

The Age of the Dinosaurs is one the many interesting attractions at LIFE Interactive World. This child is clearly taken aback at the size of this dinosaur's mouth and its big teeth.

LIFE Interactive exterior on a summer evening. The view is slightly obscured by trees.

Grey Street and the magnificent view of The Theatre Royal.

Northumberland Street. To the right is Marks & Spencer and to the left Next. In the distance is Newcastle University.

The Newcastle Civic Centre in St Mary's Place. Built in 1968, it was constructed, like many modern buildings, as ancient structures were being knocked down.

Neville Street. On the right, the splendour of the Newcastle Central Station main portico can be seen.

Percy Street, leading to Eldon Gardens and Eldon Square. The multi-storey car park is unmissable.

The peacefulness of the Newcastle Quayside in the year 2000, a far cry from the hectic days of the 1920s when ships and boats clogged these waters daily.

Local Newcastle United football hero Alan Shearer can always find time to sign autographs for the fans. Clearly popular with the youngsters, Shearer was in between takes for a TV commercial when this photograph was taken in 1999.

A tired Alan Shearer drives off home in his car after a hectic day training and filming a TV commercial. A major football match with Manchester United followed the next day.

The home of the Magpies: St James's Park, 2000. At the time this picture was taken, it was still under construction as can be seen by the crane on the left.

Barrack Road, Gallowgate. St James's Park football ground, home to Newcastle United, manager Bobby Robson and the lads. Fans make their almost religious pilgrimage here to support the Magpies.

Northumberland Road. The Pacific Bar is to the right. Parking is a major problem in Newcastle today – a contrast with the deserted streets of a century ago.

Northumberland Street, looking up the Haymarket. In the distance is Newcastle University. To the left is Index Extra. The natural stone paving blocks cost over £2 million.

Laying road surface material in Grey Street, 2000. The unmistakable Grey's Monument is straight ahead.

Marks & Spencer in the Haymarket, St Thomas' Square. The extension to Marks & Spencer was added recently.

This is the splendid, detailed sculpture at the top of the steps from the west end of the Riverside Walk. Above the sculptured head there is the arm of work and toil, signifying the number of industrial workplaces that were once in the vicinity.

The home of the world's most famous beer – Brown Ale – is the Scottish and Newcastle Breweries, pictured here at the beginning of a new century. The bronze figure of soccer legend Jackie Milburn was originally in Northumberland Street, but was moved because of a threat of vandalism.

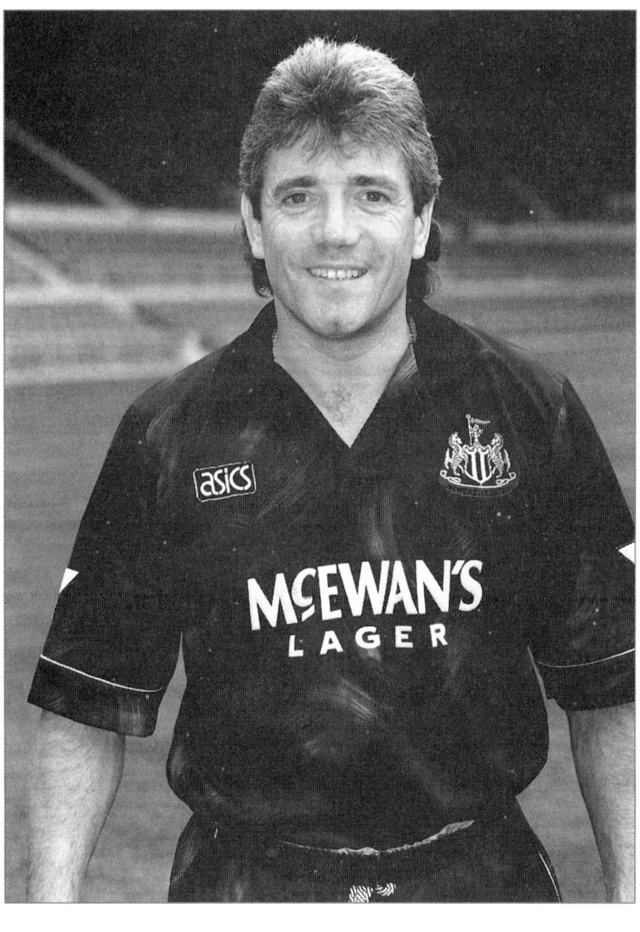

Kevin Keegan played for Newcastle United from 1982 to 1984, notching up seventy-eight appearances in the black-and-white stripe, and scoring forty-eight goals. His greatest triumph came in 1992 when he became manager. Working closely with Sir John Hall, Keegan strengthened the club, restoring its long-lost pride and hunger to win. Keegan's influence at Newcastle United is still being felt today.

FA Cup Final Home Parade, May 1999. Crowds of supporters welcome back the team after they lost 2–0 to Manchester United. A succession of similar defeats forced out manager Ruud Gullit, who was soon replaced by Bobby Robson. At his resignation press conference, Gullit talked about the pressures of managing a massive football club like Newcastle United and his relief that he could at least return to a 'normal life': 'The feeling of walking along the street minding my own business, being able to shop, being able to go to the cinema, being able to go out, being able to be like anyone else. These things seem very ordinary for someone who doesn't know what it is like to be me. These things are worth more to me than any treasure.'

Police handle the situation on the ground, as players wave to the fans in the open-top bus outside the Swallow Gosforth Park Hotel.

John Dobson Street, with the Transport and General Workers headquarters to the left, NCP car park to the right. The huge concrete tower block offers private accommodation.

Outside the Central Station, 2000, 155 years after it was opened in 1845 by Queen Victoria. It will be interesting to see how the station changes – if at all – during the next century. The message is: hang on to this book to keep a record. Hand it down through the family.

Acknowledgements and Picture Credits

Many thanks are due to: Harold and Edmund Atkinson, Newcastle United, The International Centre for LIFE, VODA International and the BUPA Great North Run, Valentine & Sons Ltd, Stephen, Jeffrey and Eva Alexander, Sid Kerr, David T. Hewitson, Sutton Commissioning Editor Simon Fletcher, WH Smith Editor Fiona Eadie, Assistant Editor Annabel Fearnley, Editor Sarah Moore, Assistant Editor Michelle Tilling, Charles Steel, Bernard Kat, Meg Colpitts, and Ronald Cooper, and Tyne and Wear Transport.

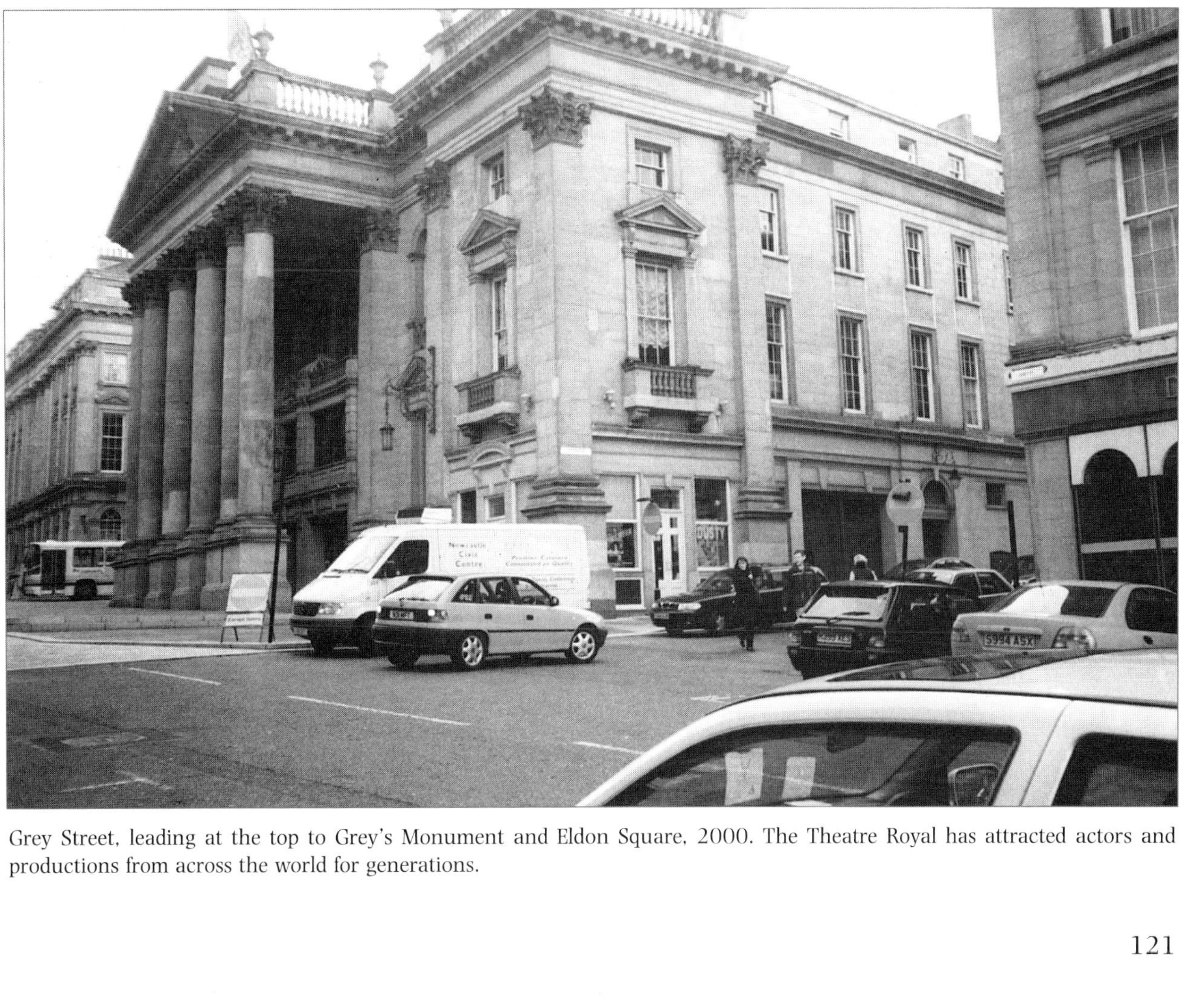

Grey Street, leading at the top to Grey's Monument and Eldon Square, 2000. The Theatre Royal has attracted actors and productions from across the world for generations.

TELEPHONE